Cats & Cocktails

ADULT COLORING BOOK

Easy Cocktail Recipes Included

Tiffany Tran

SUPPLIES NEEDED/ SIMPLE SYRUP

Hi friend!

You will need the following tools below to help you make the cocktails in this book. The recipes were thoughtfully curated to be simple to make and delicious to consume.

- Cocktail Shaker
- Cocktail Strainer
- Jigger
- Muddler
- Blender
- Pitcher

There are a few recipes that call for a few different syrup mixes. You can either make it or find it easily at your local grocery/liquor store.

Simple Syrup:

To make simple syrup, you will need a saucepan, water, and sugar. You'll want to use a ratio of one cup of water to one cup of sugar. Add the water and sugar to the saucepan and stir until the sugar is dissolved. Then, turn up the heat and bring the mixture to a simmer. Once it reaches that simmering point, remove it from the heat and let it cool. That's it! Your simple syrup is now ready to use. Keep refrigerated, and your simple syrup without any infusion is good for up to three weeks once bottled.

Honey Syrup:

To make a honey syrup, you will need a saucepan, your honey of choice, and filtered water. You'll want to use a ratio of one cup of honey to a ½ cup of water. Bring your water to a simmer and then slowly stir your honey into the water over heat until the honey has dissolved and mixture is properly combined. Remove from the heat and let it cool. Viola! Your honey syrup is ready for use. Keep refrigerated, and your honey syrup without any infusion is good for up to six weeks once bottled.

Infused Honey Syrup:

To make your infused honey syrup, you will need a saucepan, your honey of choice, your chosen fruit or herb, and filtered water. You'll want to use a ratio of one cup of honey to a ½ cup of water. Bring your water to a simmer and then slowly stir your honey into the water over heat until the honey has dissolved and mixture is properly combined. Add your fruit or herb (e.g. rosemary, etc) and remove from the heat and let it cool. Strain after two hours. Viola! Your infused honey syrup is ready for use. Keep refrigerated, and your infused honey syrup is good for up to four weeks once bottled.

FRENCH 75

Serves 1

INGREDIENTS:

1oz London Dry Gin
½oz Simple Syrup*
½oz Lemon Juice
Top with White Sparkling Wine
    (roughly 2-3oz)

RECOMMENDED
GLASSWARE:

Wine Glass

DIRECTIONS:

1. *Reference the intro page for Simple Syrup
2. Combine gin, simple syrup, lemon juice, and then add a scoop of ice into a cocktail shaker tin
3. Shake until chilled (about ten seconds) and strain into a wine glass
4. Pour a splash of your sparkling white wine over your finished cocktail
5. Garnish with a twist or peel of lemon
6. Garnish, cheers and enjoy

BEE'S KNEES

Serves 1

INGREDIENTS:

2oz Gin
1oz Lemon Juice
½oz Honey Syrup*

RECOMMENDED
GLASSWARE:

Coupe Glass

DIRECTIONS:

1. *Reference the intro page for *Honey Syrup*
2. Combine gin, honey syrup, lemon juice, and then add a scoop of ice into a cocktail shaker tin
3. Shake until chilled (about ten seconds) and strain into a coupe glass
4. Garnish with a lemon twist
5. Garnish, cheers and enjoy

DAIQUIRI

DIRECTIONS:

1. *Reference the intro page for Simple Syrup
2. Combine rum, simple syrup, lime juice, and then add a scoop of ice into a cocktail shaker tin
3. Shake until chilled (about ten seconds) and strain into your coupe or martini glass
4. Garnish with a wheel of lime
5. Garnish, cheers and enjoy

Serves 1

INGREDIENTS:

1 ½oz White Rum
1oz Lime Juice
¾oz Simple Syrup*

RECOMMENDED GLASSWARE:

Martini Glass

MEZCAL MARGARITA

Serves 1

INGREDIENTS:

2oz Tequila
1oz Lime Juice
¾oz Simple Syrup*
¼oz Orange Liqueur
(such as Cointreau or
Dry Curaçao)
¼oz of Mezcal (for your
rinse)

RECOMMENDED
GLASSWARE:

Coupe or Martini Glass

DIRECTIONS:

1. *Reference the intro page for Simple Syrup
2. Rinse your glass with Mezcal, swirling it around the glass until coated and then discard the excess
3. Combine tequila, simple syrup, lime juice, orange liqueur, and then add a scoop of ice into a cocktail shaker tin
4. Shake until chilled (about ten seconds) and strain into a coupe or martini glass
5. Garnish, cheers and enjoy

SIDECAR

Serves 1

INGREDIENTS:

1 ½oz Cognac
¾oz Orange Liqueur (such as Cointreau or
    Dry Curaçao)
¾oz Lemon Juice

RECOMMENDED GLASSWARE:

Coupe Glass

DIRECTIONS:

1. Combine gin, honey syrup, lemon juice,
   and then add a scoop of ice into a
   cocktail shaker tin
2. Shake until chilled (about ten seconds)
   and strain into a coupe or martini
   glass
3. Garnish, cheers and enjoy

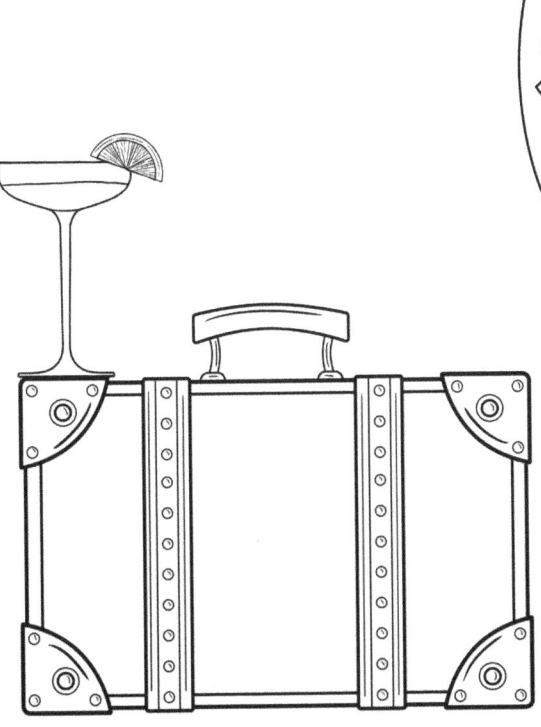

PALOMA

Serves 6

INGREDIENTS:

12oz Tequila
4.5oz Lime Juice
4.5oz Rosemary Simple Syrup*
24oz Grapefruit Soda

RECOMMENDED GLASSWARE:

Collins Glass

DIRECTIONS:

1. *Reference the intro page for *Infused Simple Syrup*
2. Take your glass and build your tequila, lime juice, and infused simple syrup and stir that with ice
3. Top with your grapefruit soda
4. Garnish, cheers, and enjoy!

OLD FASHIONED

Serves 1

INGREDIENTS:

1oz Rye
1oz Bourbon
2 dashes of Angostura bitters
2 dashes Orange bitters
¼oz Simple Syrup*

RECOMMENDED GLASSWARE:

Rocks Glass

DIRECTIONS:

1. *Reference the intro page for Simple Syrup
2. Build your rye, bourbon, Angostura bitters, orange bitters, and simple syrup into a mixing glass and add a scoop of ice, stir the mixture until chilled (about fifteen seconds)
3. Strain into your rocks glass with fresh ice
4. Garnish, cheers, and enjoy!

PISCO SOUR

Serves 1

INGREDIENTS:

1 ½oz Pisco
1oz Lemon Juice
¾oz Raspberry Simple Syrup*
1 Egg white

RECOMMENDED GLASSWARE:

Coupe Glass

DIRECTIONS:

1. *Reference the intro page for *Infused Simple Syrup*
2. Combine Pisco, raspberry simple syrup, lemon juice, and egg white to your cocktail shaker tin and "dry shake" (shake without ice) for about 20 seconds
3. Add a scoop of ice into your cocktail shaker tin and shake again
4. Shake until chilled (about ten seconds) and strain into a coupe glass
5. Garnish, cheers, and enjoy!

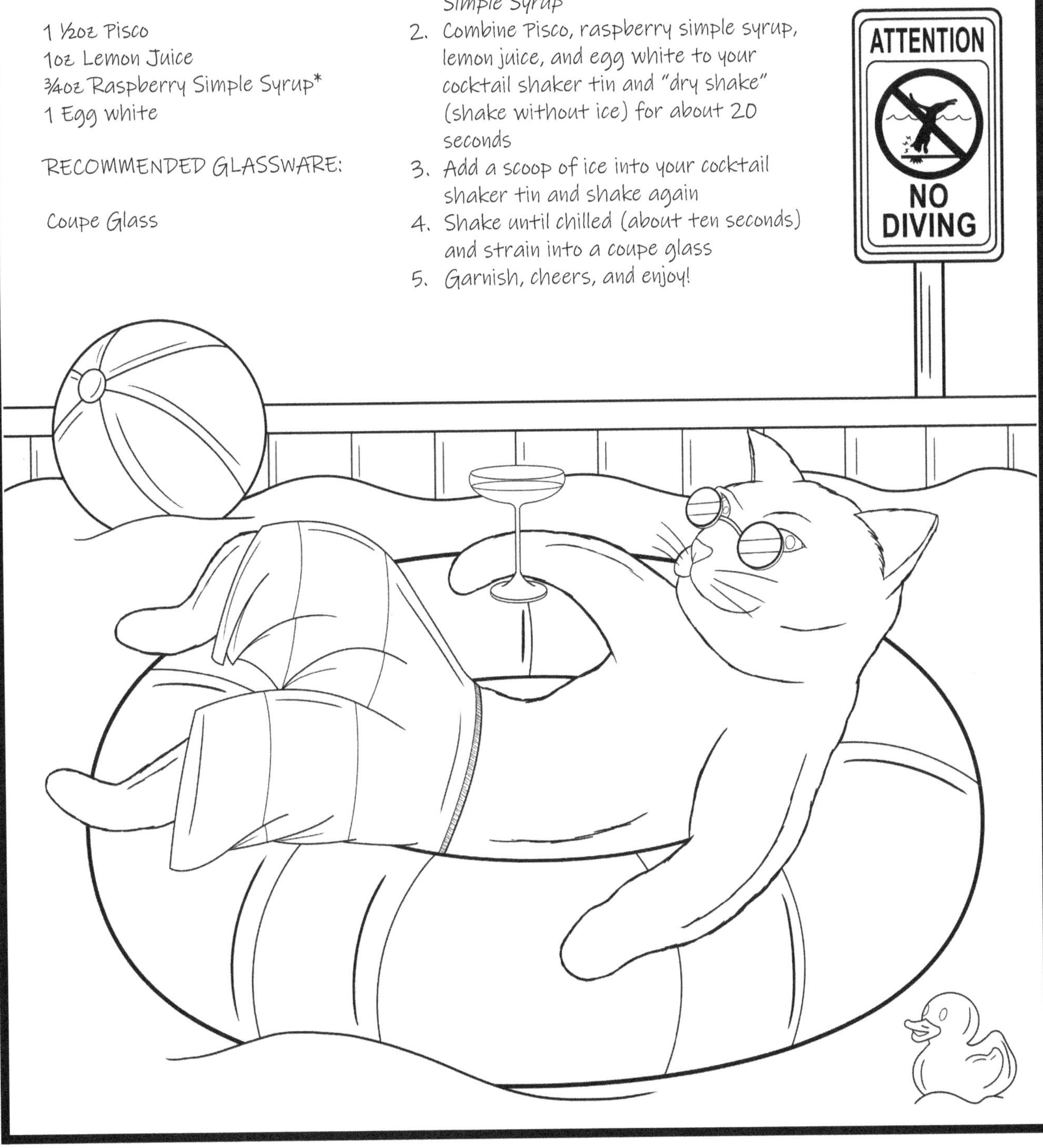

ATTENTION

NO DIVING

MARTINI

Serves 1

INGREDIENTS:

1oz Vodka
1oz London Dry Gin
½oz Dry Vermouth
1 dash Orange bitters

RECOMMENDED GLASSWARE:

Martini Glass

DIRECTIONS:

1. Build your vodka, gin, vermouth, and orange bitters into a mixing glass and add a scoop of ice, stir the mixture until chilled (about fifteen seconds) and strain into a coupe glass
2. Garnish, cheers, and enjoy!

PERFECT MANHATTAN

Serves 1

INGREDIENTS:

2oz Rye Whiskey
½oz Dry Vermouth
½oz Sweet Vermouth
3 dashes Angostura bitters

RECOMMENDED GLASSWARE:

Martini Glass

DIRECTIONS:

1. Build your rye whiskey, dry vermouth, and sweet vermouth into a mixing glass and add a scoop of ice, stir the mixture until chilled (about fifteen seconds)
2. Strain into your rocks glass with fresh ice
3. Garnish, cheers and enjoy!

Serves 1

INGREDIENTS:

2oz Gin
½oz Lime Juice
½oz Simple Syrup*
1 dash of Orange
bitters

RECOMMENDED GLASSWARE:

Coupe Glass

DIRECTIONS:

1. *Reference the intro page for Simple Syrup
2. Combine gin, simple syrup, lemon juice, and then add a scoop of ice into a cocktail shaker tin
3. Shake until chilled (about ten seconds) and strain into a coupe glass

GIMLET

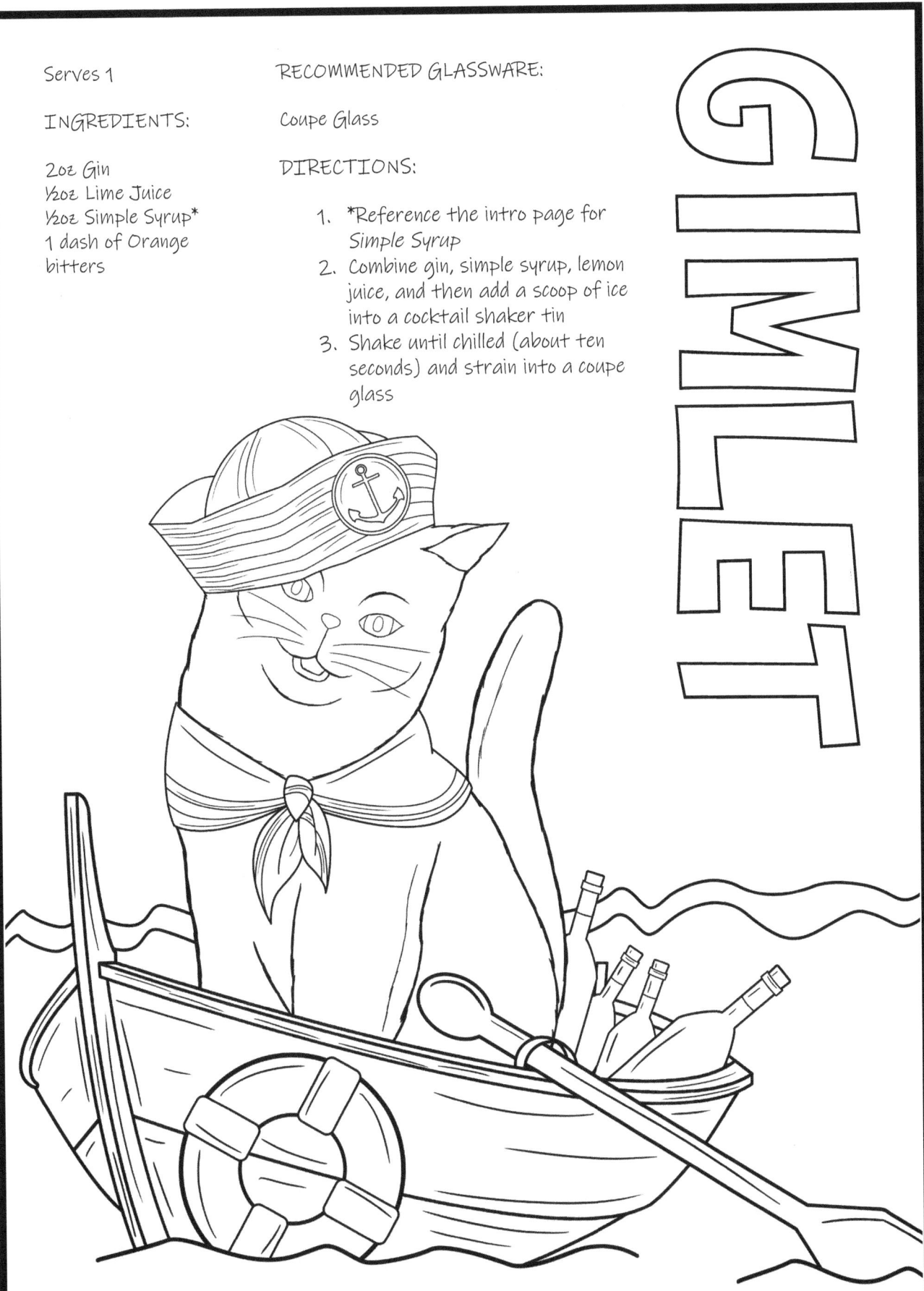

GOLD RUSH

Serves 1

INGREDIENTS:

2oz Bourbon
¾oz Lemon Juice
¾oz Rosemary-Honey Syrup*

RECOMMENDED GLASSWARE:

Rocks Glass

DIRECTIONS:

1. *Reference the intro page for *Infused Honey Syrup*
2. Combine bourbon, rosemary-honey syrup, lemon juice, and then add a scoop of ice into a cocktail shaker tin
3. Shake until chilled (about ten seconds) and strain into a coupe glass

MINT JULEP

Serves 6

INGREDIENTS:

12oz Bourbon
1.5oz Simple Syrup*
12 leaves of Mint
18 dashes of Angostura bitters

RECOMMENDED GLASSWARE:

Copper Glass or Rocks/Collins Glass

DIRECTIONS:

1. *Reference the intro page for Simple Syrup
2. Take your glass and build your bourbon, simple syrup, Angostura bitters and muddle all ingredients with the mint leaves in the bottom of a mixing glass. After, stir that mixture with ice until chilled
3. Strain mixture into your chosen glassware
4. Garnish, cheers, and enjoy!

NEGRONI

Serves 1

INGREDIENTS:

1oz Gin
1oz Campari
1oz Sweet Vermouth

RECOMMENDED GLASSWARE:

Rocks Glass

DIRECTIONS:

1. Build your gin, Campari, and sweet vermouth into a mixing glass and add a scoop of ice, stir the mixture until chilled (about fifteen seconds)
2. Strain into your rocks glass with fresh ice
3. Garnish, cheers and enjoy!

TOM COLLINS

Serves 1

INGREDIENTS:

2oz London Dry Gin
1oz Lemon Juice
½oz Simple Syrup*
2-3oz Club Soda (for your topper)

RECOMMENDED GLASSWARE:

Collins Glass

DIRECTIONS:

1. *Reference the intro page for Simple Syrup
2. Build your gin, lemon juice, and simple syrup into your glass
3. Fill with fresh ice and top with your club soda
4. Garnish, cheers and enjoy!

THE MAIN SQUEEZE

Serves 1

INGREDIENTS:

2oz Gin
½oz Maraschino
   Liqueur
¼oz Crème de
Violette
¾oz Lemon Juice

RECOMMENDED GLASSWARE:

Coupe Glass

DIRECTIONS:

1. Combine gin, maraschino liqueur, crème de violette, and lemon juice to your cocktail shaker tin
2. Shake until chilled (about ten seconds) and strain into a coupe glass
3. Garnish, cheers, and enjoy

AVIATION

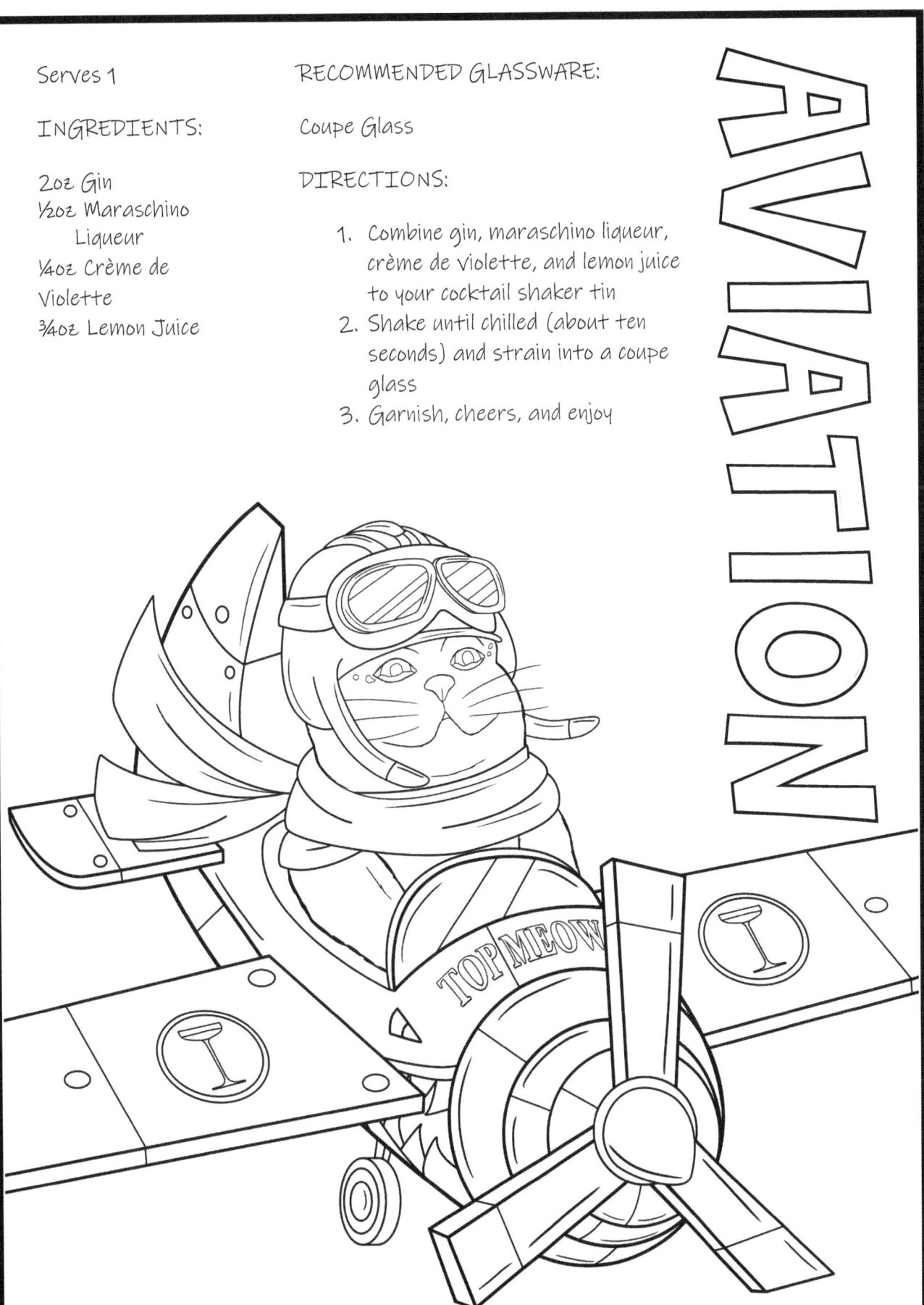

SALTY DOG

Serves 1

INGREDIENTS:

2oz your choice of either Gin or Vodka
4oz Grapefruit Juice

RECOMMENDED GLASSWARE:

Rocks Glass

DIRECTIONS:

1. Wipe a grapefruit wedge across your glass rim and dip the rim into a plate of kosher salt (the flakier the better)
2. Combine your gin or vodka with fresh grapefruit juice in your glass
3. Add fresh, crushed ice
4. Garnish with your grapefruit wedge, cheers and enjoy

CITRUS PUNCH

Serves 8

INGREDIENTS:

1 ½ cups Gin
1 cup Champagne
½ cup Cointreau
1 cup Club Soda
¾ cup Lemon Juice
½ cup Simple Syrup*
8 dashes Angostura Bitters

RECOMMENDED GLASSWARE:

Rocks Glass

DIRECTIONS:

1. *Reference the intro page for Simple Syrup
2. Build all your ingredients into a punch bowl or beverage dispenser
3. Place fresh ice in your chosen vessel
4. It's that simple!
5. Garnish, cheers and enjoy
6. If you want to kick it up a notch on the fancier side, include more fruit in the garnish. Pineapple chunks, orange slices, lemon wheels, or cinnamon sticks would love lovely floating in the mixture and would taste good, too!

MOJITO

Serves 1

INGREDIENTS:

2oz White Rum
¾oz Lime Juice
½oz Simple Syrup*
4 Mint Leaves
Club soda, as a topper

RECOMMENDED GLASSWARE:

Collins or Pint Glass

DIRECTIONS:

1. *Reference the intro page for Simple Syrup
2. Gently muddle mint leaves and your simple syrup at the bottom of a cocktail shaker tin
3. Add the rum, lime juice, and ice to your shaker and shake until chilled (about ten seconds) and strain into your glassware
4. Add fresh ice and top with club soda
5. Garnish, cheers and enjoy

Meow on me (meow on me)
Meow on me (meow on me)
I'll be gone
In a day or two

JALAPEÑO COCKTAIL

Serves 1

INGREDIENTS:

2oz Blanco Tequila
1oz Lime Juice
½oz Agave Nectar
½oz Orange Liqueur
   (Cointreau or Dry Curaçao)
2 Jalapeño Coins

DIRECTIONS:

1. Rim your glass with salt (optional)
2. Muddle your jalapeño coins in the bottom of a shaker tin
3. Add your tequila, orange liqueur, lime juice, and agave nectar with fresh ice and shake until chilled (about ten seconds) and strain into your chosen glassware
4. Garnish, cheers and enjoy

RECOMMENDED GLASSWARE:

Margarita or Coupe Glass

WATERMELON SPICE

Serves 1

INGREDIENTS:

1 ½oz Rum
¾oz Watermelon Liqueur (Dekuyper is a popular brand found just about anywhere liquor is sold, or common grocery stores)
¼oz Orange Liqueur
1oz Lime Juice
2 Pinches of Cayenne Pepper (1 if you want it with less of a kick)

RECOMMENDED GLASSWARE:

Coupe Glass

DIRECTIONS:

1. Add all your ingredients in a cocktail shaker
2. Shake until chilled (about ten seconds) and strain into your coupe glass
3. Garnish, cheers and enjoy

STRAWBERRY MOSCOW MULE

Serves 1

INGREDIENTS:

1 ½oz Vodka
½oz Simple Syrup*
½oz Lime Juice
3oz Ginger Beer
4 Strawberries

RECOMMENDED GLASSWARE:

Moscow Mule Mug

DIRECTIONS:

1. *Reference the intro page for Simple Syrup
2. Slice your strawberries and muddle the fruit at the bottom of your copper mug
3. Add your vodka, simple syrup, and lime juice into your muddled strawberries and stir thoroughly
4. Add ice and top with ginger beer
5. Garnish, cheers and enjoy

CLOVER CLUB

Serves 1

INGREDIENTS:

2oz Gin
1oz Lemon Juice
¾oz Grenadine Syrup
1 Egg white

DIRECTIONS:

1. Combine Gin, grenadine syrup, lemon juice, and egg white to your cocktail shaker tin and "dry shake" (shake without ice) for about 20 seconds
2. Add a scoop of ice into your cocktail shaker tin and shake again
3. Shake until chilled (about ten seconds) and strain into a coupe glass
4. Garnish, cheers, and enjoy!

RECOMMENDED GLASSWARE:

Coupe Glass

RASPBERRY MIMOSAS

RECOMMENDED GLASSWARE:

Champagne Flute

Serves 8

INGREDIENTS:

1 bottle of Sparkling Rosé
1 pint raspberry sorbet

DIRECTIONS:

1. Scoop 1-2 scoops of raspberry sorbet into your flute
2. Slowly top with your bubbles, the acid from the sorbet will make it bubble quite a bit but go slowly and it'll be easy!
3. Garnish, cheers and enjoy

BLUEBERRY-LEMONADE SPRITZER

RECOMMENDED GLASSWARE:

Rocks Glass

Serves 1

INGREDIENTS:

1oz Vodka
1oz Simple Syrup*
1oz Lemon Juice
1oz Champagne
2oz Sprite or another
 Lemon-Lime soda
6 Blueberries

DIRECTIONS:

1. *Reference the intro page for Simple Syrup
2. Add your blueberries and simple syrup to the bottom of your glass and muddle until mixed
3. Add the rest of your ingredients and thoroughly stir
4. Add fresh ice
5. Garnish, cheers and enjoy

TIPS & TRICKS

PRO TIPS & BAR HACKS

- If you don't have a cocktail shaker, gently "roll" your cocktail mixture with ice back and forth between any two glasses of your choice. Works like a charm in a pinch!

- Batching out your ingredients is a great way to save time mixing your drinks on a busy night. If you do so, just combine all the ingredients with proportions multiplied out by how many drinks you're anticipating on serving! An important note on this, though: If you're not planning to go through the whole batch soon then exclude the acids (any citrus or juices) so that your batch is spirit/syrup only and won't go bad as quickly.

- If you don't have a jigger or means of measurement, simply think about your cocktail in "parts" (some content even references recipes in this way) and you can use just about anything to measure things in a pinch. For example, you could use a bottle cap or spoon to help measure out the "parts" in your drink if you don't have a jigger

- Use champagne or dry sparkling wine in cocktails to instantly make sweet drinks more dry. For example, if you decide to make French 75 for a party it's too sweet and someone wants it dryer, simply splash more champagne to "dry" it up!

www.ingramcontent.com/pod-product-compliance
Lightning Source LLC
Chambersburg PA
CBHW041542120626
46551CB00019B/2799